SESAME STREET

T0016365

My Friend
JULIA

A Sesame Street Book about Autism

Jennifer Cook

Lerner Publications ◆ Minneapolis

On Sesame Street, we celebrate everyone!
All children experience the world differently
and it's important to understand, support,
and celebrate the uniqueness of each child.
Recognizing our similarities and differences
will help teach little ones to appreciate all
the wonderful things each friend brings to
their world.

Sincerely,
the Editors at Sesame Workshop

Table of Contents

Meet Julia

This is our friend Julia. She is funny, smart, and autistic.

Being autistic means she thinks and plays in her own amazing ways.

We are all a little bit different and a little bit the same.

Different and the Same

Just like Elmo and Abby, Julia loves art.

Just like Ernie, Julia loves building.

Sometimes Julia and I build things together. Sometimes we play side by side.

Julia always likes to have her bunny friend, Fluffster, with her.

When Julia feels nervous, she hugs Fluffster and feels safe.

Julia loves Fluffster. Elmo loves Baby David.

9

When Julia gets excited or nervous, she may clap and jump. She may flap her hands.

When I feel excited, I flap my super cape!

Loud sounds can bother Julia, but her headphones help quiet the noises.

Me love the sound of cookies crunching in my mouth.

When Julia's feelings get too big, she knows a way to calm herself down. She blows bubbles!

I take three deep belly breaths to calm myself down.

Some friends like hugs when they're sad. When Julia feels sad, a starfish hug can help. She spreads her fingers and touches fingertips with someone else.

When I'm sad, Julia stays with me until I feel better. She's a good friend.

Our differences are what make us amazing.
And we are all the same in one big way: we are
all friends.

Friends make me happy!

I'm happy you're our friend!

Being a Friend

There are many ways to be a friend!

- **Invite** someone new to play.

- **Show** each other how to play games.

- **Remember** that all kids play differently. If you feel confused by how a friend plays, ask them about it.

- **Take turns** doing what each of you wants to do.

- **Play** side by side if taking turns is hard. Sometimes it's nice to just keep each other company.

- **Be** patient. Take a break if you feel frustrated.

- **Show** you care. Draw a picture, share a toy, or offer a high five.

Remember that being **different** is what makes friendship great!

Glossary

autistic: having a unique way of understanding the world and other people. Autism can make it hard to figure out friends and feelings. It can also make someone caring and clever.

excited: very eager or happy

friend: someone who cares about you, spends time with you, and is kind to you

nervous: feeling a bit worried, anxious, or uncertain

Read More

Duling, Kaitlyn. *My Friend Has Autism*. Minneapolis: Jump!, 2020.

Miller, Marie-Therese. *Caring with Bert and Ernie: A Book about Empathy*. Minneapolis: Lerner Publications, 2021.

Sotomayor, Sonia. *Just Ask! Be Different, Be Brave, Be You*. New York: Philomel Books, 2019.

Index

Photo Acknowledgments

Image credits: FatCamera/E+/Getty Images, pp. 20, 21 (bottom left); PeopleImages/iStock/ Getty Images, p. 21 (top right).

About the Author

Jennifer Cook was identified as being on the autism spectrum in 2011, just after her three children were also diagnosed. She is the author of eight best-selling books in eight languages, has advised at the White House and National Institutes of Health, appeared on Netflix's *Love on the Spectrum*, and sits on the Autism Society of America's Council of Autistic Advisors.

For my children

Lerner Publications Company
An imprint of Lerner Publishing Group, Inc.
241 First Avenue North
Minneapolis, MN 55401 USA

For reading levels and more information, look up this title at www.lernerbooks.com.

Main body text set in Mikado.
Typeface provided by HVD.

Editor: Amber Ross **Designer:** Laura Otto Rinne
Photo Editor: Annie Zheng
Lerner Team: Martha Kranes

Library of Congress Cataloging-in-Publication Data

Names: Cook, Jennifer, 1975- author.
Title: My friend Julia : A Sesame Street book about autism / Jennifer Cook.
Description: Minneapolis : Lerner Publications, [2024] | Includes bibliographical references and index. | Audience: Ages 4–8 | Audience: Grades K–1 | Summary: "We are all amazing because we are all different. Abby, Elmo, and the Sesame Street friends introduce young readers to Julia. Full-color photos and accessible text make this book an age-appropriate introduction to autism"— Provided by publisher.
Identifiers: LCCN 2022035573 (print) | LCCN 2022035574 (ebook) | ISBN 9781728486710 (library binding) | ISBN 9781728499109 (ebook)
Subjects: LCSH: Autism—Juvenile literature. | Autistic children—Juvenile literature.
Classification: LCC RJ506.A9 C6685 2024 (print) | LCC RJ506.A9 (ebook) | DDC 618.92/85882—dc23/eng/20220831

LC record available at https://lccn.loc.gov/2022035573
LC ebook record available at https://lccn.loc.gov/2022035574

Manufactured in the United States of America
1-52616-50790-10/19/2022